THE HISTORY OF WING CHUN:
PHILOSOPHY AND IMPACT OF A MARTIAL ARTS LEGACY

What You Need to Know About Its Origins, Principles, and Cultural Influence

By

Leighton Tokunbo Shepherd

Copyright Page

The History of Wing Chun: Philosophy and Impact of a Martial Arts Legacy

Copyright © 2024 by Leighton Tokunbo Shepherd
All rights reserved.

No part of this book may be reproduced, distributed, or transmitted in any form or by any means, including photocopying, recording, or other electronic or mechanical methods, without the prior written permission of the author, except in the case of brief quotations embodied in critical reviews and certain other noncommercial uses permitted by copyright law.

For permissions, contact:
Leighton Tokunbo Shepherd
Beijing, China

This is a work of nonfiction. The stories and examples are based on the author's experiences, observations, and interpretations. The publisher and author are not responsible for any actions taken as a result of this book.

Book Description

What This Book Brings to Your Journey

This book isn't just a deep analysis into Wing Chun—it's a story about its origins, evolution, and the lasting impact it has on people's lives. Whether you're here to learn the techniques, explore the philosophy, or understand its global influence, this guide offers something for everyone. It's designed to give you a clear and meaningful understanding of what makes Wing Chun so special, both as a martial art and a way of life.

Key Chapters and Discoveries

Introduction: Why Wing Chun Matters

- Explore why Wing Chun resonates across generations and cultures.
- Learn what makes it more than just a martial art—it's a practice of focus and simplicity.

Chapter 1: Origins of Wing Chun

- Discover the humble beginnings of Wing Chun and the legends that surround its creation.
- See how history shaped its techniques and philosophy.

Chapter 2: Evolution Through the Ages

- Follow Wing Chun's journey from its roots to its many modern interpretations.
- Understand how it has adapted to meet the needs of each new generation.

Chapter 3: Philosophy at the Core

- Learn about the deep philosophical values that define Wing Chun, like balance, efficiency, and mindfulness.
- See how these principles apply to life outside the practice.

Chapter 4: Wing Chun Techniques in Practice

- Break down the techniques that make Wing Chun unique, from swift strikes to smooth trapping moves.

- Understand the "why" behind its focus on precision and economy of movement.

Chapter 5: Wing Chun's Cultural Impact

- Discover how Wing Chun has influenced martial arts, movies, and culture worldwide.
- Learn about its connection to famous figures like Bruce Lee.

Chapter 6: Wing Chun in a Changing World

- See how Wing Chun is used in modern self-defense and everyday challenges.
- Explore how technology and changing times are helping preserve its rich traditions.

Chapter 7: Wing Chun Beyond Combat

- Find out how Wing Chun builds confidence, mindfulness, and resilience.
- Learn how its teachings help people grow, face challenges, and strengthen relationships.

Chapter 8: Notable Figures in Wing Chun History

- Meet the legends and pioneers who shaped Wing Chun into what it is today.
- Explore their stories and their dedication to keeping the art alive.

Chapter 9: The Global Reach of Wing Chun

- See how Wing Chun has spread across the world and inspired people from all walks of life.
- Hear stories of practitioners and how the art has connected them across cultures.

Chapter 10: Why Wing Chun Continues to Resonate

- Understand why Wing Chun remains practical, inspiring, and timeless in today's world.
- Discover how its principles continue to shape lives everywhere.

Afterword: Carrying Wing Chun Forward

- Reflect on the importance of keeping Wing Chun authentic while embracing change.

- Explore how its future depends on community, teaching, and sharing its values.

This book is an invitation to explore Wing Chun—its history, its people, and its enduring lessons. Whether you're just starting your journey or have practiced for years, it offers insights that will inspire you to see Wing Chun not just as a martial art, but as a tool for living with purpose and intention.

table of Contents

By...1
Leighton Tokunbo Shepherd...1
What This Book Brings to Your Journey..................................4
Key Chapters and Discoveries..4
table of Contents..10
    Introduction: Why Wing Chun Matters.................................14
    Chapter 1: Origins of Wing Chun..17
    Chapter 2: Evolution Through the Ages...............................24
    Chapter 3: Philosophy at the Core..31
    Chapter 4: Wing Chun Techniques in Practice.....................36
    Chapter 5: Wing Chun's Cultural Impact..............................43
    Chapter 6: Wing Chun in a Changing World.......................49
        Wing Chun in Modern Self-Defense..............................49
        The Role of Technology...51
        Preserving Tradition..52
        Wing Chun in Popular Culture......................................53
        Wing Chun and Personal Development........................54
        The Future of Wing Chun..55
        A Legacy of Resilience..56
    Chapter 7: Wing Chun Beyond Combat...............................57
        Building Confidence Through Practice..........................57
        The Role of Mindfulness..58
        Wing Chun as a Path to Discipline................................59
        Adapting to Life's Challenges.......................................60
        Strengthening Relationships...62
        A Tool for Personal Growth...63
        The Legacy of Wing Chun Beyond Combat..................64
    Chapter 8: Notable Figures in Wing Chun History...............65
        The Founding Legends...65
        The Guardians of Tradition..67
        The First Steps Toward Openness................................68
        The Pioneers of Modern Wing Chun.............................69
        The Modern Ambassadors...70

- Preserving the Legacy 71
- The Human Connection 72

Chapter 9: The Global Reach of Wing Chun 73
- Wing Chun's Spread Across Continents 73
- The Role of Teachers 74
- A Universal Appeal 75
- Cultural Exchange Through Wing Chun 76
- Challenges of Globalization 77
- Stories from Practitioners Around the World 78
- The Future of Wing Chun 80

Chapter 10: Why Wing Chun Continues to Resonate 82
- Practicality That Speaks to Everyone 82
- A Connection Between Body and Mind 84
- Personal Growth Through Discipline 85
- A Global Community 86
- A Tradition That Evolves 87
- Why Wing Chun Feels So Timeless 88

Afterword: Carrying Wing Chun Forward 90
- Passing the Torch 90
- The Importance of Authenticity 91
- Reaching New Audiences 92
- Embracing Technology 93
- The Role of Community 94
- Why Wing Chun Matters 95
- The Endless Journey 96

Appendix: Resources for Exploring Wing Chun 98
- Finding a School 98
- Online Resources 99
- Recommended Reading 100
- Events and Seminars 101
- Training Equipment 102
- Advice for Beginners 102

Staying Inspired.. 103

Introduction: Why Wing Chun Matters

Wing Chun is a martial art with roots buried deep in history. It's not about mysticism or flashy moves; it's a practical, efficient, and direct fighting style that has endured for centuries because it works. Developed during a time of conflict and change, Wing Chun emerged as a way for people to defend themselves, not through brute strength, but through precision, strategy, and technique.

The story begins in southern China during the Qing Dynasty. According to legend, Wing Chun was created by a Shaolin nun named Ng Mui. She designed this system to help Yim Wing Chun, a young woman, defend herself against an aggressive suitor. The system was built on principles of simplicity and efficiency, using body mechanics and positioning to outmaneuver stronger opponents. While the legend is debated, the practicality of Wing Chun remains undisputed.

Unlike many martial arts that focus on broad, sweeping techniques or large, open movements, Wing Chun thrives in close quarters. It's about controlling the centerline, delivering fast, precise strikes, and neutralizing threats quickly. This made it an ideal choice for the bustling, narrow alleyways and densely packed communities where it was practiced and passed down.

Over time, Wing Chun grew from a localized self-defense system to an internationally recognized martial art. Its reach expanded significantly thanks to notable practitioners like Ip Man, who refined and popularized the art in Hong Kong. He taught a generation of students, including Bruce Lee, who would go on to influence martial arts on a global scale.

Today, Wing Chun is practiced all over the world, not just for its self-defense applications, but because of its adaptability and focus on technique over brute strength. It's a martial art that anyone can learn, regardless of age, size, or physical ability.

This book isn't about romanticizing Wing Chun or placing it on a pedestal. It's about understanding the reality of its history, the practicality of its techniques, and the way it has evolved over time. From its origins to its influence on modern martial arts, this is the story of Wing Chun told as it truly is—an enduring and effective martial art rooted in simplicity, adaptability, and precision.

If you're curious about where Wing Chun came from, how it works, and why it continues to resonate with martial artists worldwide, you're in the right place. Let's dive in.

Chapter 1: Origins of Wing Chun

When I first started learning about Wing Chun's history, I didn't expect to be drawn into a world of mystery, rebellion, and survival. I figured it was just another martial art with an interesting backstory. But the more I dug, the more I realized Wing Chun wasn't just a product of its time—it was a response to it. The world in which this art was born wasn't easy. It was turbulent, filled with political unrest, and shaped by the need to survive against overwhelming odds.

Let's set the scene. We're in Southern China, sometime during the late 1600s to early 1700s. The Qing Dynasty is in power, and it's not exactly a peaceful reign. The government is clamping down hard on dissenters, especially those who might be connected to the remnants of the Ming Dynasty. People are caught between loyalty to the past and the harsh realities of the present. It's in this environment that martial arts were more than just exercises or skills—they were tools for survival.

Now, this is where things get a little murky. Like a lot of ancient traditions, Wing Chun's origins are wrapped in legend. The story that's often told starts with a Buddhist nun named Ng Mui. According to the tale, she was one of the Five Elders of the Shaolin Temple—people who escaped the destruction of the temple during a Qing attack. Ng Mui was said to be a brilliant martial artist, but she knew that brute force and brute strength weren't always the answer.

Here's what I find so fascinating about her supposed role in Wing Chun's creation. The legend says she developed the art after observing a fight between a snake and a crane. She saw how the snake's movements were efficient, striking directly, while the crane relied on deflection and precise angles. That observation became the foundation of Wing Chun's techniques—direct, efficient, and grounded in practicality.

But here's the thing: while the legend of Ng Mui might not be historically verifiable, it carries a deeper truth. Wing Chun wasn't about brute strength or flashy moves. It was about creating a system that worked, even for someone who wasn't the biggest or strongest person in the room. That idea—developing a martial art that anyone could use—feels revolutionary to me.

Then there's the story of Yim Wing Chun, the young woman who the art is named after. The story goes that Yim Wing Chun was being harassed by a local warlord who demanded she marry him. She agreed to fight him in a duel, saying she would marry him if he won. With the techniques she learned from Ng Mui, she defeated him. It's a dramatic story, and while we can't be sure of its historical accuracy, it paints a vivid picture of Wing Chun as an art designed for the underdog.

What really strikes me about these stories—whether they're completely true or just part of the art's mythology—is how much they reflect the principles of Wing Chun itself. This is a martial art for people who need to be efficient and resourceful. It's not about overpowering your opponent; it's about outthinking and outmaneuvering them.

Now, let's talk about the historical context. This was a time when martial arts were often practiced in secret. The Qing government didn't exactly look kindly on groups of people training in combat skills, especially when those skills could potentially be used against them. So, martial artists had to be careful. They trained in secluded places, passing their knowledge down through small, trusted circles.

Wing Chun developed in this environment of secrecy and necessity. It wasn't a system you learned over years and years of training. It was designed to be practical and fast to learn. If you were in trouble, you needed something that worked immediately—not a style that required decades to master. That's part of why Wing Chun focuses so much on close-range combat. It's about surviving in situations where there's no room for error.

What's interesting to me is how these historical realities shaped not just the techniques but the philosophy of Wing Chun. Take the idea of simplicity, for example. In a time when life was unpredictable and often dangerous, the art's creators didn't have the luxury of overcomplicating things. They distilled martial arts down to their most effective elements, cutting out anything that didn't serve a clear purpose.

And then there's the principle of adaptability. Wing Chun teaches you to flow with your opponent's energy, to react in real time rather than relying on pre-planned techniques. This mirrors the lives of the people who created it—they had to be adaptable, finding ways to survive in a world that was constantly changing.

As Wing Chun grew, it began to spread beyond its original circles. At first, it was passed down through a few trusted disciples. These were people who weren't just learning techniques; they were being entrusted with a system of knowledge that had been honed through real-world experience. Over time, those disciples started teaching others, and the art began to take on a life of its own.

One of the most remarkable things about Wing Chun's history is how it managed to survive through so many generations. Think about it: this was a time before the internet, before books on martial arts were widely available, before global communication was even a possibility. The fact that Wing Chun was passed down, preserved, and eventually shared with the world is nothing short of incredible.

When I think about those early practitioners, I can't help but admire their dedication. They weren't just learning a martial art; they were preserving a piece of their culture, their history, and their identity. That sense of responsibility is something that still resonates with me today.

By the time Wing Chun started to spread internationally, it had already been refined over generations. Each teacher added their own insights, building on the foundations laid by their predecessors. And yet, despite all these changes, the core principles remained the same. Wing Chun's simplicity, efficiency, and practicality continued to shine through.

As I look back on its origins, I'm struck by how much Wing Chun reflects the resilience of the people who created it. This wasn't just about fighting—it was about surviving, adapting, and finding strength in the face of adversity. That's what makes its history so compelling to me. It's not just a story about a martial art; it's a story about human ingenuity and determination.

Wing Chun's origins might be shrouded in legend, but the truths behind those stories are real. This is an art born from necessity, shaped by the challenges of its time, and preserved by the dedication of its practitioners. And as we continue to explore its history, philosophy, and impact, I think you'll see just how much there is to learn from this remarkable martial art.

Chapter 2: Evolution Through the Ages

Wing Chun's journey from the secretive hands of its earliest practitioners to becoming a global martial art is nothing short of remarkable. Its evolution tells a story of resilience, adaptation, and a steadfast commitment to preserving its essence despite the currents of change. Understanding this journey means delving into history, not just the dates and events but the human element—the choices, risks, and sacrifices that kept Wing Chun alive through centuries of turmoil.

To understand how Wing Chun evolved, you must first appreciate its beginnings. This was not a system developed in peacetime or for sport. It came into existence during an era of rebellion and suppression, in the shadows of a fractured China under Qing rule. The very act of practicing or teaching martial arts was, at times, a political statement. Early Wing Chun practitioners were individuals who understood that knowledge could be as dangerous as a weapon and as valuable as gold.

Wing Chun's growth from these secretive roots was gradual, marked by an unbroken chain of dedication. This art wasn't passed down to large classes or publicly demonstrated in grand halls. It was taught in whispers, shared in hidden spaces, and entrusted only to those deemed worthy. Small groups of students would learn directly from a teacher, not just the physical movements but the principles behind them—principles that were as much about survival as they were about combat.

But what kept Wing Chun alive wasn't just secrecy. It was its adaptability. Unlike some martial arts that rely heavily on tradition for tradition's sake, Wing Chun has always been pragmatic. If something worked, it was kept. If something didn't, it was discarded. This practicality ensured that the art stayed relevant, even as the world around it changed.

As the political landscape of China shifted, so too did Wing Chun's circumstances. By the 19th century, the art had started to find its way beyond the secluded villages of Southern China. Merchants, laborers, and travelers began carrying its teachings into the cities. Among the most significant environments for Wing Chun's spread were the bustling marketplaces and docks. Here, physical confrontations were a reality of daily life, and the close-quarters techniques of Wing Chun proved invaluable.

What's important to grasp is that this wasn't a passive evolution. Every time Wing Chun moved into a new context, it adapted. Techniques were refined based on the needs of the practitioners, whether they were tradesmen defending themselves from thieves or workers looking for a way to navigate the rougher aspects of urban life. The art didn't lose its core; it adjusted, growing stronger through practical use.

The transition from secretive tradition to urban survival marked a critical point in Wing Chun's history. It wasn't just being preserved; it was being tested. Every confrontation, every lesson taught in dimly lit backrooms or crowded docks, added to the art's development. In this period, Wing Chun transformed from a tightly held system into something dynamic and evolving, shaped by the realities of those who practiced it.

In the early 20th century, Wing Chun's evolution took another leap forward. A handful of practitioners began teaching the art more openly, albeit cautiously. This was an era of change in China, where martial arts were beginning to emerge from the shadows. Schools were being established, and systems that had once been taught in whispers were now being shared with broader audiences. Wing Chun, however, remained selective in its dissemination. Teachers were careful about who they entrusted with its knowledge, holding onto the belief that the art was more than just a series of techniques. It was a legacy.

One of the most intriguing aspects of Wing Chun's development during this period was the diversity of its students. People from different walks of life came to learn, each bringing their own perspectives and needs. Some were martial artists looking to expand their knowledge. Others were individuals seeking a practical means of self-defense. The result was a blending of experiences that enriched the art without diluting its core.

The mid-20th century marked a turning point in Wing Chun's story. For the first time, the art began to reach an international audience. Migrants carried it overseas, and teachers who had once confined their instruction to small, local circles began to teach it in new lands. This expansion was not without its challenges. In a world increasingly driven by commercialization, there was a risk that Wing Chun's depth and philosophy might be overshadowed by its more marketable aspects.

But Wing Chun proved resilient. Its principles of efficiency and adaptability were not just techniques—they were part of the art's DNA. Teachers who carried it abroad found ways to preserve its essence while introducing it to students from vastly different cultures. This required not just skill but an understanding of the art's deeper meanings. They weren't just teaching movements; they were transmitting a philosophy, one that emphasized precision, mindfulness, and the importance of staying grounded even in the face of external chaos.

As Wing Chun spread globally, it began to take on new forms. Practitioners in the West, for example, often approached it with a focus on practicality and self-defense, while others delved into its philosophical underpinnings, exploring how its principles could apply to everything from personal development to business strategies. This diversity of interpretation was both a challenge and a strength. It showed how versatile the art could be, but it also raised questions about how much could be adapted before Wing Chun lost its identity.

Today, Wing Chun stands at an interesting crossroads. It's more widely known than ever before, with schools and practitioners in nearly every corner of the world. Yet, its growth has brought with it debates about authenticity. What does it mean to practice Wing Chun "correctly"? Can the art evolve without losing its roots? These are questions that every generation of practitioners has faced, and they are not easily answered.

What I find most compelling about Wing Chun's evolution is that it reflects a broader truth about human resilience. Just as the art adapted to new challenges, so too have its practitioners. They've found ways to preserve its principles while embracing change, ensuring that Wing Chun remains not just relevant but vital.

The history of Wing Chun is not just a story of techniques or traditions. It's a story of people—of teachers who risked everything to pass on their knowledge, of students who used what they learned to overcome adversity, and of communities that found strength and identity through the art. It's a reminder that what we inherit from the past is not static. It's alive, growing and changing with each generation.

Chapter 3: Philosophy at the Core

Wing Chun isn't just a collection of moves or a method for self-defense. At its heart, it's a philosophy—a way of thinking that informs how practitioners move, react, and even live their lives. To understand the art fully, you have to go beyond the punches and kicks. You have to delve into the ideas that form its foundation.

What sets Wing Chun apart from so many other martial arts is its commitment to simplicity and efficiency. These aren't just buzzwords—they're principles rooted in a way of life. The philosophy of Wing Chun emerged not from abstract theory but from necessity. In its earliest days, when survival depended on quick thinking and practical action, these principles weren't just helpful—they were essential.

One of the most defining concepts in Wing Chun is the centerline theory. Imagine a line running vertically down the middle of your body, dividing it into two halves. This centerline represents your core, your balance, and your most vulnerable areas. Wing Chun teaches you to protect this line at all costs while simultaneously targeting your opponent's. It's a straightforward idea, but it carries immense weight.

What makes the centerline theory so impactful is how it connects the physical to the mental. In combat, staying centered means maintaining your balance and structure. But in life, it means holding onto your values and priorities, even when external forces try to pull you in different directions. This dual application of the centerline—both in fighting and in everyday life—is one of the reasons Wing Chun resonates so deeply with its practitioners.

Another key principle in Wing Chun is the idea of economy of motion. In practical terms, this means avoiding unnecessary movements. Why throw a wide punch when a straight one will do? Why waste energy with flourishes when directness is more effective? This principle isn't just about fighting—it's a reflection of a broader mindset. It's about cutting through distractions and focusing on what really matters.

I've often thought about how this principle applies outside the training hall. Life is full of complexities and competing demands, but Wing Chun's emphasis on simplicity teaches us to strip away the excess and focus on the essentials. It's a lesson that feels timeless, even in our modern, fast-paced world.

Wing Chun also emphasizes relaxation—something that might seem counterintuitive in a martial art. But in Wing Chun, tension is your enemy. A tense body is a slow body, one that reacts poorly under pressure. By staying relaxed, you move more fluidly, respond more quickly, and conserve energy. This principle reflects a deep understanding of the human body and mind, one that feels remarkably ahead of its time.

In many ways, the philosophy of Wing Chun mirrors the lives of the people who created it. They lived in an unpredictable world, one where challenges came at close range, without warning. Their art reflects that reality. It's about staying calm under pressure, responding efficiently, and never overcommitting to a single course of action.

The idea of adaptability is another cornerstone of Wing Chun's philosophy. Practitioners are taught to flow with their opponent's energy rather than fighting against it. If someone pushes, you pull. If someone pulls, you push. This principle isn't just about combat—it's a way of approaching challenges in life. Instead of resisting change, Wing Chun teaches you to adapt and use it to your advantage.

There's also a philosophical humility to Wing Chun. Unlike some martial arts that emphasize dominance or overwhelming power, Wing Chun is about understanding your limits and working within them. It's not about proving how strong or skilled you are—it's about being effective. This humility is reflected in the way practitioners approach their training, always seeking to improve, refine, and learn.

For many practitioners, the philosophy of Wing Chun extends far beyond the training hall. It shapes how they interact with the world, how they approach challenges, and how they think about themselves. The lessons of Wing Chun—stay centered, move efficiently, remain adaptable—are as relevant in the workplace or at home as they are in a fight.

One of the most beautiful aspects of Wing Chun's philosophy is how accessible it is. You don't need to be a philosopher or a scholar to understand it. Its principles are simple, clear, and grounded in reality. They're the kind of lessons that anyone can relate to, whether they're a seasoned martial artist or someone stepping onto the mat for the first time.

Over the years, I've seen how these principles have impacted people's lives. I've met students who came to Wing Chun looking for self-defense but found something much deeper—a sense of clarity, confidence, and calm. I've seen how the art's emphasis on balance and adaptability has helped people navigate personal and professional challenges.

But what's most striking to me is how timeless these principles feel. The world has changed so much since Wing Chun was first developed, but its lessons remain relevant. In a way, that's a testament to the wisdom of its creators. They weren't just developing a fighting system; they were crafting a philosophy that could withstand the test of time.

Chapter 4: Wing Chun Techniques in Practice

If Wing Chun's philosophy is its soul, then its techniques are the body through which that soul moves. The techniques of Wing Chun are unlike those of most martial arts you might encounter. They are designed to be practical, adaptable, and efficient, but behind every movement lies a deeper principle—a lesson about focus, precision, and the relationship between power and control. To truly understand the art, one must not only study its movements but also the ideas that give those movements their meaning.

The first thing anyone learns in Wing Chun is how to stand. That might sound almost laughably basic—after all, how hard could standing be? But in Wing Chun, the stance is everything. It's called the Yee Gee Kim Yeung Ma, or the "character two" stance, named for its resemblance to the Chinese character for the number two. Feet are turned slightly inward, knees bent, and weight distributed evenly. To someone unfamiliar with Wing Chun, it might look awkward or even unnatural. But spend a little time in this stance, and you'll quickly realize its purpose: stability.

The stance is designed to root you to the ground, providing a solid base from which all other movements flow. Without a stable stance, nothing else in Wing Chun works. It teaches you to remain balanced, both literally and metaphorically. In combat, balance keeps you grounded, preventing you from being easily toppled. In life, it reminds you to stay centered, even when the world feels like it's shifting beneath your feet.

Once the stance is mastered—or at least understood—the next step is learning how to move. This is where Wing Chun really starts to challenge your perception of what a martial art should look like. Movements in Wing Chun are small, controlled, and deliberate. There's no leaping, no spinning, no dramatic flourishes. You move forward when there's an opening, retreat when there's danger, and sidestep when the situation calls for it.

What's remarkable is how these movements are designed to conserve energy. In Wing Chun, every step, every shift of weight, serves a purpose. The art doesn't ask you to outlast your opponent through sheer endurance. Instead, it teaches you to outthink and outmaneuver them, using your energy efficiently and effectively.

From movement, we transition to the hands—the tools of Wing Chun. The open palm strikes, straight punches, and deflections are all carefully calculated to deliver maximum impact with minimum effort. The straight punch, for instance, is one of the most iconic techniques in Wing Chun. Delivered along the centerline, it's direct and powerful, designed to reach the target in the shortest time possible.

But what makes the straight punch so effective isn't just its speed or power—it's the way it embodies Wing Chun's philosophy. The punch isn't just an attack; it's a statement of intent. It says, "I see the target, and I will reach it in the most efficient way possible." This principle of directness carries over into everything Wing Chun teaches, from blocking to counterattacking to footwork.

One of the most unique and challenging aspects of Wing Chun is Chi Sao, or "sticky hands." If you've ever watched a Wing Chun demonstration, you've probably seen two practitioners standing close together, their arms in constant motion as they engage in what looks like a choreographed dance. But Chi Sao is anything but choreographed.

The purpose of Chi Sao is to train sensitivity—the ability to feel your opponent's intentions through touch. In a fight, you might not always be able to see what's coming, especially in close quarters. Chi Sao teaches you to rely on your sense of touch, responding to your opponent's movements almost instinctively. It's a drill, but it's also a mindset. You're not just reacting; you're flowing, adapting, and staying connected.

For me, Chi Sao was one of the most humbling parts of learning Wing Chun. It's not about brute force or overpowering your partner. In fact, the more force you use, the less effective you become. Chi Sao demands relaxation, focus, and a willingness to listen—not with your ears, but with your body. It's a physical conversation, one where every movement is a question or an answer.

Wing Chun also places a heavy emphasis on structure. The arms, for example, are often held in a guard position known as the Wu Sao (protecting hand) and the Fook Sao (bridging hand). These positions are not just defensive; they're active, constantly seeking opportunities to deflect attacks and create openings. The idea is to protect your centerline while staying ready to attack at a moment's notice.

Blocking in Wing Chun isn't about brute force; it's about redirection. When an attack comes, you don't meet it head-on. Instead, you guide it away, using angles and leverage to neutralize the threat. This principle of redirection is one of the art's most powerful tools. It's a reminder that you don't always have to fight force with force. Sometimes, the smartest move is to step aside and let the attack miss its mark.

The wooden dummy, or Muk Yan Jong, is another iconic tool in Wing Chun training. It's more than just a piece of equipment; it's a partner, a mirror that reflects your strengths and weaknesses. Practicing on the wooden dummy helps you refine your movements, improve your accuracy, and develop a deeper understanding of angles and positioning.

What's fascinating about the wooden dummy is how it forces you to confront your habits. Are your punches too wide? Is your stance unstable? The dummy doesn't lie. It reveals every flaw in your technique, challenging you to correct it. Over time, training with the wooden dummy becomes less about the equipment itself and more about the self-awareness it fosters.

One of the most rewarding aspects of Wing Chun is how everything comes together. The stance, the movement, the strikes, the blocks—they're all interconnected, part of a larger system that operates as a whole. When you see a skilled practitioner in action, it's like watching a symphony. Every movement flows into the next, each one precise and purposeful.

But Wing Chun isn't just about mastering techniques. It's about understanding the principles behind them and applying those principles in real-world situations. It's about learning to trust your instincts, stay calm under pressure, and move with intention.

For many practitioners, the techniques of Wing Chun become a metaphor for life. The way you stand reflects your confidence. The way you move reflects your adaptability. And the way you strike reflects your clarity of purpose.

As we delve deeper into Wing Chun's techniques, keep in mind that they're more than just physical movements. They're expressions of a philosophy, a way of thinking that can shape not only how you fight but how you approach the world. In the next chapter, we'll explore the cultural impact of Wing Chun, looking at how this art has touched lives and influenced communities around the globe.

Chapter 5: Wing Chun's Cultural Impact

Wing Chun has never been just a martial art. Its roots may lie in self-defense and survival, but over the centuries, it has evolved into a cultural symbol—a representation of resilience, adaptability, and philosophy in motion. While its techniques are studied and practiced across the globe, its cultural significance is often overlooked. Wing Chun's journey from the small villages of Southern China to the global stage is a testament not just to its practicality but to the values it represents.

To understand the cultural impact of Wing Chun, we need to start with its beginnings. In its earliest days, Wing Chun was a martial art practiced in secrecy, often by those on the fringes of society. These weren't elite warriors training in palaces or schools. They were villagers, laborers, and rebels who needed a practical and reliable system to defend themselves. Wing Chun wasn't designed to impress; it was designed to survive.

But even in those early days, the art carried deeper meanings. It wasn't just about fighting—it was about empowerment. For people who were often marginalized or oppressed, Wing Chun provided a way to stand their ground, both physically and metaphorically. It became a quiet form of resistance, a way to reclaim a sense of agency in a world that often tried to strip it away.

As the art spread beyond its origins, it began to take on new cultural dimensions. By the late 19th and early 20th centuries, Wing Chun had moved into urban centers, where it found a home among a broader range of practitioners. Merchants, dock workers, and even members of the emerging middle class began to embrace the art. It was during this period that Wing Chun started to become more than a martial art—it became a cultural touchstone.

One of the reasons Wing Chun resonated so deeply with people was its accessibility. Unlike some other martial arts, which often required years of physical conditioning or specialized training, Wing Chun was straightforward. Its techniques could be learned relatively quickly and applied effectively, even by those without prior experience. This practicality made it appealing to people from all walks of life, allowing it to transcend social and economic boundaries.

At the same time, Wing Chun retained its philosophical depth. The principles of balance, simplicity, and adaptability weren't just tools for combat—they were lessons for life. Practitioners found that the same skills they used in the training hall could help them navigate challenges in their personal and professional lives. This duality—practicality combined with philosophy—gave Wing Chun a unique place in the cultural landscape.

By the mid-20th century, Wing Chun had started to gain international attention. Migrants carried the art to new countries, teaching it in small, informal settings. In many cases, these teachers weren't trying to spread Wing Chun for fame or fortune; they were simply sharing a part of their heritage. But as more people began to encounter the art, its reputation grew.

One of the pivotal moments in Wing Chun's cultural journey came with its influence on film and media. While avoiding specific trademarked names or figures, it's impossible to ignore how cinema brought Wing Chun into the public eye. The portrayal of Wing Chun on screen introduced the art to millions of viewers, many of whom had never encountered it before. These depictions often emphasized the art's elegance, efficiency, and philosophical underpinnings, creating a sense of intrigue and admiration among audiences worldwide.

The impact of these portrayals was profound. For many, Wing Chun became a symbol of discipline, focus, and strength. It wasn't just about fighting—it was about how one carried oneself in the face of adversity. The art's emphasis on staying calm under pressure and using energy efficiently resonated with people in ways that extended far beyond the training hall.

As Wing Chun gained popularity, schools began to emerge in cities around the world. These schools weren't just places to learn techniques—they became cultural hubs, where people from different backgrounds came together to study, train, and share ideas. For many practitioners, learning Wing Chun was as much about connecting with a rich cultural tradition as it was about mastering self-defense.

The global spread of Wing Chun also led to its adaptation in new and unexpected ways. In some places, the art became a tool for personal development, with teachers emphasizing its philosophical lessons as much as its physical techniques. In others, it was embraced as a practical system for self-defense, tailored to the needs of modern urban environments.

But as Wing Chun grew, it also faced challenges. The commercialization of martial arts brought with it the risk of dilution—of losing the depth and meaning that had made the art so special in the first place. Some schools focused on teaching flashy techniques, neglecting the principles and philosophy that underpinned them. This tension between tradition and modernization became a defining feature of Wing Chun's cultural journey.

Despite these challenges, Wing Chun has continued to thrive. Its ability to adapt while staying true to its core principles is one of the reasons it remains so relevant today. Whether practiced in a traditional setting or a modern gym, the art still carries the same lessons of balance, simplicity, and adaptability.

In many ways, Wing Chun's cultural impact extends beyond the people who practice it. The art has influenced how we think about movement, discipline, and even conflict resolution. Its emphasis on staying calm under pressure and responding with precision has found applications in fields as diverse as leadership, education, and therapy.

For many practitioners, Wing Chun is more than just a hobby—it's a way of life. The lessons learned in the training hall often spill over into everyday experiences, shaping how people approach challenges, interact with others, and carry themselves. This holistic impact is one of the reasons why Wing Chun continues to resonate with so many people.

As we reflect on Wing Chun's cultural journey, it's clear that the art's significance goes far beyond its techniques. It's a living, breathing tradition, one that continues to evolve and inspire. And as it moves into the future, Wing Chun remains a powerful reminder of the values that connect us—balance, focus, and the pursuit of mastery.

Chapter 6: Wing Chun in a Changing World

As we move further into the 21st century, Wing Chun stands at an interesting crossroads. It's no longer just a small, niche martial art practiced in the secretive confines of Chinese villages or urban back alleys. Instead, it's become a global phenomenon, embraced by people from all walks of life and corners of the world. But with this growth comes the challenge of balancing tradition with modernity. How does an ancient art form like Wing Chun remain relevant in a world that's moving faster and becoming more interconnected every day?

To answer that, we need to look at how Wing Chun has adapted to modern challenges without losing the essence of what makes it special. This isn't just about teaching new techniques or using better equipment; it's about understanding the changing needs of practitioners and finding ways to meet them.

Wing Chun in Modern Self-Defense

One of the biggest ways Wing Chun has adapted to the modern world is by focusing on self-defense. Let's face it, most people don't walk into a martial arts school these days looking to prepare for a duel or a battlefield. They're looking for something practical—something that can help them feel safer in their daily lives.

And that's where Wing Chun shines. Its close-range techniques, quick strikes, and focus on efficiency make it an incredibly effective system for self-defense. Unlike some other martial arts that require years of practice to master, Wing Chun's principles can be applied relatively quickly. Practitioners learn to assess threats, respond instinctively, and neutralize danger with minimal effort.

In urban environments, where space is limited, and threats can appear suddenly, Wing Chun's close-quarters combat techniques are particularly useful. You don't need a lot of room to defend yourself effectively; in fact, the art is specifically designed for situations where you're up close and personal with an attacker.

But modern self-defense isn't just about physical techniques. It's also about awareness and mindset. Many

Wing Chun schools today teach situational awareness as part of their curriculum, helping students recognize potential threats and avoid dangerous situations altogether. It's a holistic approach that goes beyond the physical, emphasizing the importance of staying calm, focused, and prepared.

The Role of Technology

Another way Wing Chun has adapted to the modern world is through the use of technology. In the past, learning Wing Chun often meant finding a local teacher and attending in-person classes. While that's still an important part of the learning process, technology has opened up new possibilities for how the art is taught and shared.

Online tutorials, video courses, and virtual training sessions have made Wing Chun more accessible than ever before. For someone living in a remote area with no local schools, this can be a game-changer. They can study the basics, practice drills, and even get feedback from instructors without leaving their home.

Of course, there are limits to what you can learn online. The tactile nature of Wing Chun—the way it emphasizes sensitivity and touch—means that in-person training is still invaluable. But technology has created opportunities for more people to get started, and for advanced practitioners to connect with teachers and peers across the globe.

Preserving Tradition

While adapting to modernity is important, so is preserving the traditions and values that make Wing Chun unique. This is where things can get tricky. As the art grows and evolves, there's always the risk of losing sight of its roots. Some schools focus heavily on teaching flashy techniques or emphasizing speed over substance, diluting the art's depth in the process.

But many practitioners are deeply committed to preserving Wing Chun's essence. For them, it's not just about learning how to fight—it's about understanding the philosophy and principles that underpin the art. They see themselves as stewards of a tradition, responsible for passing it on to the next generation in a way that honors its history.

This balance between tradition and innovation is one of the most fascinating aspects of modern Wing Chun. On the one hand, the art must evolve to stay relevant. On the other hand, it must remain true to itself. Striking that balance requires a deep understanding of what Wing Chun is and what it stands for.

Wing Chun in Popular Culture

Another way Wing Chun has found relevance in the modern world is through its presence in popular culture. Over the years, the art has appeared in movies, TV shows, and even video games, introducing it to millions of people who might not otherwise have encountered it. These portrayals often highlight Wing Chun's elegance, efficiency, and philosophical depth, creating a sense of intrigue and admiration among audiences.

However, popular culture can be a double-edged sword. While it's helped bring Wing Chun into the mainstream, it's also led to some misconceptions about the art. Many people see only the cinematic version of Wing Chun, with its perfectly choreographed fight scenes and larger-than-life heroes. While these portrayals are entertaining, they don't always reflect the reality of what Wing Chun is or what it can do.

For practitioners, this can be both an opportunity and a challenge. On the one hand, popular culture has brought more attention to Wing Chun, attracting new students and spreading awareness of the art. On the other hand, it's up to the teachers and schools to help students move beyond the surface and discover the deeper aspects of the art.

Wing Chun and Personal Development

One of the most powerful ways Wing Chun has adapted to modern life is by serving as a tool for personal development. More and more people are discovering that the lessons learned in the training hall—focus, discipline, adaptability—have applications far beyond self-defense.

In a world that often feels chaotic and overwhelming, Wing Chun provides a sense of grounding. Its emphasis on balance, both physical and mental, helps practitioners navigate challenges with clarity and confidence. The principles of economy of motion and efficiency aren't just about fighting—they're about making better choices, managing time and energy, and approaching life with purpose.

For some, Wing Chun becomes a form of moving meditation. The repetitive practice of forms, the focus required in Chi Sao (sticky hands), and the precision of techniques all encourage mindfulness. In this way, Wing Chun becomes not just a physical practice but a mental and emotional one as well.

The Future of Wing Chun

As we look to the future, the question remains: how will Wing Chun continue to evolve? The world is changing faster than ever, and martial arts are not immune to these shifts. But if history has taught us anything, it's that Wing Chun is remarkably adaptable.

One possibility is that Wing Chun will continue to expand into new areas, finding applications in fields like leadership training, conflict resolution, and even therapy. Its principles of focus, adaptability, and balance are universal, making them relevant in nearly any context.

At the same time, it's likely that Wing Chun will face new challenges, from maintaining its authenticity to finding ways to engage younger generations. But if the art's history is any indication, it will rise to the occasion.

A Legacy of Resilience

Ultimately, Wing Chun's ability to adapt while staying true to its core is what has allowed it to thrive for so long. It's a testament to the resilience of the art and the people who practice it. Whether it's being used for self-defense, personal growth, or cultural connection, Wing Chun continues to make an impact in the modern world.

Chapter 7: Wing Chun Beyond Combat

Wing Chun, while deeply rooted in practical self-defense, extends far beyond its martial application. It's a philosophy, a way of thinking, and for many, a way of life. The techniques that make Wing Chun an efficient system for close-range combat also serve as metaphors for navigating challenges, finding balance, and achieving personal growth. In this chapter, we'll explore the ways Wing Chun transcends the physical, touching aspects of the mind, spirit, and daily life.

Building Confidence Through Practice

One of the most immediate benefits people notice when they start practicing Wing Chun is an increase in confidence. But this isn't the loud, boastful confidence that comes from being able to throw a punch. It's quieter, steadier—a sense of self-assurance that comes from truly understanding your own capabilities.

Think about the first time you faced a situation you weren't sure you could handle. Maybe it was a presentation at work, a difficult conversation with a loved one, or stepping into an unfamiliar environment. Now imagine having a toolkit that not only prepared you for those moments but made you feel calm and collected while facing them. That's what Wing Chun does for many of its practitioners.

The art doesn't just teach you how to react; it teaches you how to trust yourself. The repetitive practice of drills, forms, and techniques might seem mundane at first, but it builds a deep reservoir of confidence. Each time you successfully block a strike, maintain your balance, or execute a precise movement, you're proving to yourself that you can handle what's in front of you. Over time, this mindset spills over into other areas of life, making you more prepared to face challenges of all kinds.

The Role of Mindfulness

Mindfulness has become a bit of a buzzword in recent years, but in Wing Chun, it's more than just a concept—it's a practice. The art demands total presence. You can't half-heartedly perform a movement or let your mind wander while practicing Chi Sao. Every drill, every form, every application requires your full attention.

This focus on the present moment can be incredibly grounding. In today's world, where distractions are everywhere, Wing Chun provides a rare opportunity to step away from the noise and focus entirely on what you're doing. It's not just about punching or blocking; it's about being fully engaged with your body, your breath, and your surroundings.

For many practitioners, this mindfulness becomes one of the most valuable aspects of their training. It helps them stay centered in stressful situations, whether they're on the mat or in the middle of a hectic day. It's not about shutting out the world; it's about being fully present in it, responding with clarity and purpose instead of reacting out of panic or habit.

Wing Chun as a Path to Discipline

Discipline is often seen as a difficult or unpleasant thing—something you do because you have to, not because you want to. But in Wing Chun, discipline feels different.

It's not about forcing yourself to train or sticking to a rigid routine. It's about finding joy and purpose in the process.

The structured nature of Wing Chun's practice naturally fosters discipline. Each form builds on the one before it, requiring patience and persistence to master. You can't skip ahead or rush through the basics; they're the foundation upon which everything else is built. This process teaches you to appreciate small, incremental progress and to value the effort it takes to improve.

But what's truly transformative is how this discipline extends beyond the training hall. Practitioners often find that the habits they develop in their Wing Chun practice—patience, consistency, and attention to detail—start showing up in other areas of their lives. Whether it's tackling a project at work, pursuing a personal goal, or maintaining relationships, the discipline learned through Wing Chun becomes a valuable tool.

Adapting to Life's Challenges

One of Wing Chun's core principles is adaptability. In combat, this means flowing with your opponent's energy instead of resisting it, finding ways to use their strength against them. But this principle isn't limited to fighting—it applies to every aspect of life.

Life is unpredictable. Challenges and obstacles can appear out of nowhere, and rigid plans often fall apart. Wing Chun teaches you to embrace this uncertainty instead of fearing it. By staying flexible and open to change, you can navigate even the most difficult situations with grace and confidence.

I've heard countless stories from practitioners who credit Wing Chun with helping them through tough times. One friend of mine, for example, told me how the principles of balance and adaptability he learned in Wing Chun helped him recover from a serious injury. Instead of feeling defeated by the setback, he approached his recovery with the same mindset he used in training—adjusting his approach, staying patient, and focusing on what he could control.

Another student shared how Wing Chun helped her deal with workplace stress. She found that the lessons she learned about staying calm under pressure and responding thoughtfully instead of reacting impulsively were invaluable when dealing with difficult colleagues and high-pressure deadlines.

These stories highlight one of Wing Chun's most powerful qualities: its ability to prepare you not just for physical confrontations but for the challenges of daily life.

Strengthening Relationships

At first glance, it might not seem like a martial art has much to do with relationships. But Wing Chun, with its emphasis on connection and communication, can actually teach you a lot about how to relate to others.

Take Chi Sao, for example. This training drill, often called "sticky hands," is all about sensitivity and responsiveness. You're not trying to overpower your partner; you're trying to understand their movements and intentions through touch. This requires a level of awareness and presence that translates surprisingly well to relationships.

Think about how often misunderstandings or conflicts arise because we're not really paying attention to the other person. We're caught up in our own thoughts, assumptions, or emotions, and we miss what they're trying to communicate. Wing Chun teaches you to slow down, to listen—not just with your ears, but with your whole being.

This practice of mindfulness and sensitivity can deepen your connections with others, whether it's a partner, a friend, or a colleague. It's not about agreeing with everything they say or avoiding conflict—it's about being present and responsive, creating a space where genuine understanding can take place.

A Tool for Personal Growth

Perhaps the most profound way Wing Chun extends beyond combat is as a tool for personal growth. It's not just about becoming a better fighter—it's about becoming a better version of yourself.

Wing Chun challenges you to confront your weaknesses, whether they're physical, mental, or emotional. It asks you to be honest with yourself about where you are and what you need to improve. But it also gives you the tools to make that improvement, one step at a time.

For some, this journey is about building physical strength or improving coordination. For others, it's about overcoming self-doubt, managing stress, or finding a sense of purpose. Whatever the goal, Wing Chun provides a framework for growth that's both practical and deeply meaningful.

The beauty of this process is that it's never really finished. There's always more to learn, more to refine, more ways to grow. This sense of ongoing exploration is part of what makes Wing Chun so rewarding. It's not just a skill you master; it's a lifelong journey.

The Legacy of Wing Chun Beyond Combat

When you step back and look at the bigger picture, it's clear that Wing Chun's impact extends far beyond the training hall. It's a tool for self-defense, yes, but it's also a path to self-discovery, a guide for navigating life's challenges, and a source of connection and community.

In a world that often feels chaotic and overwhelming, Wing Chun offers something rare: a sense of balance, focus, and control. It reminds us that strength isn't just about power—it's about clarity, adaptability, and resilience.

Chapter 8: Notable Figures in Wing Chun History

Wing Chun's journey from a secretive martial art practiced in hidden corners of Southern China to a global phenomenon didn't happen by chance. It was shaped by the dedication, ingenuity, and vision of the individuals who practiced, preserved, and passed it on. These figures, though separated by time and geography, share a common thread: their belief in the power and relevance of Wing Chun.

This chapter is dedicated to those who contributed to the art's growth and evolution, from the mythical origins to the practitioners of today. It's not just about recognizing names or tracing a lineage—it's about understanding the human element behind Wing Chun's legacy. These stories remind us that Wing Chun is not just a set of techniques or principles; it's a living tradition, carried forward by people who believed in its potential.

The Founding Legends

The origins of Wing Chun are shrouded in myth and folklore, and while the historical accuracy of these tales is debated, their cultural and symbolic significance is undeniable.

At the heart of the legend is the figure of Ng Mui, a Buddhist nun who is said to have been one of the Five Elders who escaped the destruction of the Shaolin Temple. According to the story, Ng Mui developed the foundation of Wing Chun after observing a fight between a snake and a crane. She saw the snake's directness and precision and the crane's ability to deflect and evade, combining these qualities into a new martial art.

Ng Mui's student, Yim Wing Chun, is another pivotal figure in the legend. As the story goes, Yim Wing Chun was a young woman who used the techniques taught by Ng Mui to fend off a local warlord who sought to force her into marriage. Her victory not only preserved her autonomy but also demonstrated the practicality and effectiveness of the art, which would later bear her name.

While these stories may lack historical evidence, they encapsulate the essence of Wing Chun. They remind us that the art was born out of necessity, designed for real-world challenges, and rooted in the idea that skill and strategy can triumph over brute strength.

The Guardians of Tradition

As Wing Chun moved from myth into history, it was preserved and refined by generations of practitioners who dedicated their lives to the art. These early teachers were often unsung heroes, working in relative obscurity to ensure that Wing Chun was not lost.

Unlike some martial arts that developed in formal schools or academies, Wing Chun was passed down through small, trusted circles. Teachers selected their students carefully, prioritizing character and commitment over physical ability. This selective approach wasn't just about preserving the art—it was about protecting it. In an era when martial arts were often suppressed or viewed with suspicion, secrecy was a matter of survival.

These early practitioners didn't have the resources or tools we take for granted today. There were no training manuals, videos, or standardized curriculums. Everything was taught through demonstration and repetition, with each teacher adding their own insights and refinements. Despite these limitations, or perhaps because of them, the art flourished.

The First Steps Toward Openness

The 19th and early 20th centuries marked a turning point for Wing Chun. During this period, the art began to emerge from the shadows and gain recognition outside its traditional circles.

One of the reasons for this shift was the changing social and political landscape in China. As cities grew and communities became more interconnected, martial artists began to share their knowledge more openly. Wing Chun, with its practical techniques and adaptable philosophy, found a receptive audience among workers, merchants, and others seeking an effective system for self-defense.

Teachers who were once bound by tradition began to take on more students, expanding the reach of Wing Chun while still maintaining its core principles. This delicate balance—between preserving the art's integrity and adapting to the needs of a changing world—set the stage for Wing Chun's eventual global spread.

The Pioneers of Modern Wing Chun

By the mid-20th century, Wing Chun was poised to make its mark on the international stage. This period saw the emergence of influential teachers who played a crucial role in popularizing the art and bringing it to new audiences.

These pioneers often faced significant challenges. They had to navigate cultural differences, adapt their teaching methods to suit students from diverse backgrounds, and contend with the commercialization of martial arts. Despite these obstacles, they succeeded in preserving the essence of Wing Chun while making it accessible to a broader audience.

One key development during this era was the establishment of formal schools. Unlike the small, private training sessions of the past, these schools allowed for larger classes and a more structured approach to teaching. They also provided a space for students to connect with one another, creating a sense of community that remains a hallmark of Wing Chun to this day.

The Modern Ambassadors

Today, Wing Chun is practiced and taught by thousands of people around the world. Modern instructors continue to adapt the art to meet the needs of their students while staying true to its principles.

One of the defining features of modern Wing Chun is its diversity. Practitioners come from all walks of life, each bringing their own perspectives and experiences to the art. Some focus on its combat applications, while others are drawn to its philosophy or its potential for personal growth.

The global nature of Wing Chun has also led to new innovations and interpretations. Practitioners have developed training tools, integrated Wing Chun with other martial arts, and even applied its principles to fields like leadership, education, and therapy. This ongoing evolution is a testament to the art's adaptability and relevance in the modern world.

Preserving the Legacy

While Wing Chun continues to grow and evolve, there is also a strong commitment among practitioners to preserve its roots. This isn't always easy. As the art spreads and diversifies, there is always a risk of losing sight of its origins.

To address this, many teachers emphasize the importance of understanding Wing Chun's history and philosophy. They encourage students to study not just the techniques but the principles and values that underpin them. This holistic approach ensures that Wing Chun remains more than just a set of movements—it remains a way of thinking and a way of life.

The Human Connection

What strikes me most about Wing Chun's history is how deeply human it is. This is an art that has been shaped, preserved, and carried forward by people—ordinary men and women who saw its value and dedicated themselves to its practice.

Their stories remind us that Wing Chun isn't just about combat or technique. It's about resilience, adaptability, and the belief that with focus and determination, we can overcome any challenge.

Chapter 9: The Global Reach of Wing Chun

Today, Wing Chun is a global phenomenon, practiced and studied in nearly every corner of the world. From small, traditional training halls in rural villages to bustling urban studios filled with students of all backgrounds, the art has transcended its humble beginnings. But this global reach didn't happen overnight. It's the result of centuries of dedication, adaptation, and, most importantly, the human connections that have carried Wing Chun across borders and cultures.

Wing Chun's Spread Across Continents

The spread of Wing Chun beyond China began with migration. During the 19th and early 20th centuries, many Chinese communities emigrated to Southeast Asia, Europe, and the Americas, bringing their traditions and cultural practices with them. Martial arts were an integral part of these communities, both as a means of self-defense and as a way to preserve their cultural identity in foreign lands.

Initially, Wing Chun remained within these communities, taught quietly to small groups of students. It wasn't something widely advertised or practiced publicly, often due to the challenges of assimilation and the desire to protect the art's integrity. However, over time, as these communities established themselves, Wing Chun began to emerge from the shadows.

One of the key reasons Wing Chun resonated with people outside of its traditional circles was its accessibility. Unlike some martial arts that require years of rigorous physical conditioning or acrobatic skills, Wing Chun's techniques are based on efficiency and natural movement. This made it appealing to a diverse range of practitioners, from young children to older adults, from complete beginners to experienced martial artists looking to expand their knowledge.

The Role of Teachers

The global spread of Wing Chun owes much to the teachers who took it upon themselves to share the art with the world. These individuals often faced significant challenges, from language barriers to cultural differences, but their passion and dedication ensured that the art found new homes far from its origins.

What's remarkable about these teachers is how they adapted their methods to suit their students while maintaining the integrity of the art. In Europe, for example, Wing Chun schools began to incorporate structured curriculums, emphasizing the theoretical and philosophical aspects of the art alongside physical training. In the Americas, many instructors tailored their classes to focus on self-defense, reflecting the practical concerns of urban environments.

These adaptations weren't about changing Wing Chun—they were about making it accessible without losing its essence. The teachers understood that the art's core principles—efficiency, adaptability, and balance—were universal, even if the way they were taught needed to be adjusted for different audiences.

A Universal Appeal

What makes Wing Chun so universally appealing? Part of it is its practicality. In a world where people are often looking for effective self-defense methods, Wing Chun offers a system that works. Its close-range techniques, quick strikes, and focus on real-world applications make it relevant in nearly any context.

But Wing Chun's appeal goes beyond its practicality. It's also a deeply philosophical art, one that encourages practitioners to think critically, stay calm under pressure, and approach challenges with clarity and purpose. These qualities resonate with people from all walks of life, whether they're martial artists, professionals, or simply individuals looking to improve themselves.

For many, Wing Chun becomes more than just a martial art—it becomes a way of living. The lessons learned in the training hall often spill over into other areas of life, helping practitioners navigate everything from personal relationships to professional challenges. This holistic impact is one of the reasons why Wing Chun continues to attract students from such diverse backgrounds.

Cultural Exchange Through Wing Chun

One of the most interesting aspects of Wing Chun's global reach is how it has become a vehicle for cultural exchange.

In every country where it's practiced, Wing Chun brings together people from different backgrounds, fostering connections and mutual understanding.

In some cases, this cultural exchange happens directly in the training hall. Students learn not just the techniques of Wing Chun but also the history, philosophy, and cultural values that underpin the art. For many, this is their first exposure to Chinese culture, providing a window into a rich and complex tradition.

In other cases, the exchange is more subtle. Practitioners bring their own perspectives and experiences to the art, creating a dialogue between Wing Chun's traditional principles and modern, global realities. This dialogue enriches the art, ensuring that it continues to grow and evolve while staying rooted in its origins.

Challenges of Globalization

Of course, the globalization of Wing Chun hasn't been without its challenges. As the art has spread, it has faced issues of commercialization, dilution, and even competition among schools. In some cases, the emphasis on attracting students has led to a focus on flashy techniques or quick results, at the expense of the deeper principles that make Wing Chun so meaningful.

This isn't a new problem—martial arts have always had to balance tradition with adaptation—but it's one that requires constant vigilance. For many teachers and practitioners, the solution lies in education. By emphasizing the history and philosophy of Wing Chun alongside its techniques, they ensure that students gain a deeper understanding of what the art truly represents.

Another challenge is the question of authenticity. With so many schools and interpretations of Wing Chun, how do you know what's "real"? This question often sparks heated debates among practitioners, but the truth is, there's no single answer. Wing Chun has always been a living art, shaped by the people who practice it. What matters most is not whether a school adheres to a specific lineage or style but whether it embodies the principles and values that define Wing Chun.

Stories from Practitioners Around the World

To truly understand the global reach of Wing Chun, it's worth hearing from the practitioners themselves. Their stories offer a glimpse into how the art has touched lives in ways that go far beyond the training hall.

I once met a practitioner from Brazil who had started Wing Chun as a way to recover from a difficult period in his life. For him, the art wasn't just about learning to fight—it was about finding a sense of balance and purpose. He told me how the principles of Wing Chun, particularly its emphasis on adaptability, helped him navigate the challenges he faced in his personal and professional life.

Another practitioner from Germany shared how Wing Chun had helped her overcome a fear of confrontation. As a small-framed woman, she had always felt vulnerable in situations where she might have to defend herself. But through Wing Chun, she learned to trust her instincts and rely on technique rather than brute strength. For her, the art was empowering in a way that extended far beyond physical self-defense.

And then there was the student from Canada who was drawn to Wing Chun for its philosophical depth. A lifelong martial artist, he found that Wing Chun's emphasis on mindfulness and efficiency complemented his existing training while offering new insights into how to approach challenges. For him, Wing Chun wasn't just another style—it was a framework for thinking and living.

The Future of Wing Chun

As we look to the future, it's clear that Wing Chun's global journey is far from over. The art continues to grow, reaching new audiences and adapting to new challenges. But what will the next chapter of Wing Chun's story look like?

Some practitioners believe that technology will play an increasingly important role, making the art more accessible to people in remote areas. Others see opportunities for Wing Chun to be integrated into fields like education, therapy, and leadership training, where its principles can have a broader impact.

What's certain is that Wing Chun will continue to evolve, just as it has for centuries. Its ability to adapt while staying true to its core principles is what has allowed it to thrive, and that adaptability will ensure its relevance in the years to come.

At its heart, Wing Chun is more than just a martial art—it's a testament to the power of human connection. It's a bridge between past and present, between teacher and student, and between people from all walks of life. Its global reach is a reminder that, no matter where we come from or what challenges we face, we all share a common desire for growth, understanding, and connection.

Chapter 10: Why Wing Chun Continues to Resonate

Wing Chun isn't just a martial art; it's an experience that seems to stay with people long after their first punch, block, or stance. You hear it in the way practitioners talk about their training—it's not just about mastering the physical techniques but also about how those lessons seep into the rest of their lives. What's remarkable about Wing Chun is how it continues to resonate with people from all walks of life, no matter where they come from or why they start practicing.

This chapter is about exploring why Wing Chun has this staying power. What is it about this art that makes people stick with it, talk about it, and share it with others? From its practical self-defense techniques to its deep philosophy and personal growth potential, Wing Chun offers something that feels timeless and universal.

Practicality That Speaks to Everyone

One of the first things people notice about Wing Chun is how practical it is. Unlike some martial arts that can feel overly complicated or designed for sport, Wing Chun is straightforward. It's built for real-life situations.

Take, for example, the way it handles attacks. In Wing Chun, you don't waste time with flashy movements or unnecessary force. If someone throws a punch, you block it with just enough energy to redirect it and then follow up with a counterstrike. It's efficient, quick, and direct.

This practicality is one of the reasons people from so many different backgrounds are drawn to Wing Chun. You don't need to be particularly athletic, strong, or even young to start learning. The techniques are designed to work with your natural abilities, making them accessible to almost anyone.

For people who want to feel safer or more confident in their ability to protect themselves, Wing Chun offers a level of reassurance that's hard to find elsewhere. The moves are simple, but they work—and that's what makes all the difference.

A Connection Between Body and Mind

While Wing Chun is undoubtedly practical, it's also deeply philosophical. This is something that surprises many beginners. They come in expecting to learn how to throw punches, but they leave with lessons that go far beyond the physical.

One of the core principles of Wing Chun is staying centered—both physically and mentally. In the training hall, this means maintaining your balance and protecting your centerline. But outside of training, it becomes a metaphor for life. How do you stay grounded when everything around you feels chaotic? How do you keep your priorities in focus when distractions are pulling you in every direction?

Practicing Wing Chun teaches you to find that balance. It's not something you master overnight, but over time, you start to notice how the lessons from training seep into your everyday life. You might find yourself reacting more calmly in stressful situations or approaching challenges with a clearer head.

It's this connection between the body and mind that keeps many practitioners coming back. They're not just learning how to fight—they're learning how to live with more intention and focus.

Personal Growth Through Discipline

There's a certain kind of growth that happens when you practice something consistently over time. In Wing Chun, this growth comes not just from mastering techniques but from the discipline the art demands.

Let's be honest—learning Wing Chun isn't always easy. The movements might seem simple at first glance, but perfecting them takes time and effort. There are days when you feel like you're making progress and days when it feels like you're stuck. But that's part of the process.

What's incredible is how this discipline starts to shape you. It teaches you patience—how to stick with something even when it feels challenging. It teaches you humility—how to accept feedback and recognize that there's always more to learn. And it teaches you resilience—how to keep going, even when things don't go as planned.

For many people, these lessons extend far beyond the training hall. They find themselves applying the same discipline to other areas of their lives, whether it's at work, in relationships, or while pursuing personal goals. Wing Chun becomes a tool for self-improvement, one that helps them become better versions of themselves.

A Global Community

Another reason Wing Chun continues to resonate is the sense of community it creates. No matter where you go in the world, you can find people who share a passion for this art.

One of the most rewarding aspects of practicing Wing Chun is connecting with others who are on the same journey. In the training hall, you're not just learning from your teacher—you're learning from your training partners as well. Every drill, every sparring session, is an opportunity to grow together.

This sense of connection often extends beyond the physical space of the school. Practitioners from different backgrounds and cultures share their experiences, ideas, and insights, creating a global network of people united by their love for the art.

For many, this community becomes like a second family. It's a space where they feel supported, challenged, and inspired—a reminder that they're not alone in their journey.

A Tradition That Evolves

One of the most remarkable things about Wing Chun is how it manages to honor its traditions while continuing to evolve. This balance between the old and the new is part of what keeps the art so relevant.

At its core, Wing Chun is rooted in principles that have stood the test of time—balance, efficiency, adaptability. These principles are as applicable today as they were hundreds of years ago. But the way they're taught and applied has changed to meet the needs of modern practitioners.

For example, many schools now incorporate discussions about situational awareness and modern self-defense scenarios. Teachers adapt their methods to suit students from different cultures, age groups, and levels of experience.

This willingness to evolve is one of the reasons Wing Chun continues to resonate. It's not a static art frozen in the past—it's a living tradition that grows and changes with the people who practice it.

Why Wing Chun Feels So Timeless

Ultimately, what makes Wing Chun so enduring is its universality. At its heart, it's about solving problems—whether those problems are physical, mental, or even philosophical.

It's about learning how to stay grounded when life feels unstable, how to move efficiently when things get complicated, and how to respond thoughtfully instead of reacting impulsively. These are lessons that never go out of style.

For many practitioners, Wing Chun becomes a lifelong journey. It's not just something they do—it's something they live. And that's why it continues to resonate, generation after generation.

As we wrap up this exploration of Wing Chun, it's clear that the art's impact goes far beyond its techniques. It's a way of thinking, a way of being, and a reminder that with focus, balance, and adaptability, we can face whatever challenges come our way.

Afterword: Carrying Wing Chun Forward

Writing about Wing Chun is like trying to capture the ocean in a single photograph—it's impossible to show everything all at once. The art is too vast, too layered, too personal to be confined to a few words on a page. For those who practice it, Wing Chun is not just a skill or a discipline; it's a lifelong journey, a connection to something greater than themselves.

As we come to the end of this exploration, one question remains: where does Wing Chun go from here? What's next for this art that has already traveled so far and touched so many lives? The answer, I believe, lies in the hands of its practitioners—those who carry its traditions, its principles, and its philosophy into the future.

Passing the Torch

Wing Chun's survival has always depended on the people who practice it. From its earliest days, it was passed down from teacher to student, generation after generation. This isn't an art that's been preserved in books or museums—it's been kept alive through human connection, through the physical and philosophical lessons shared between individuals.

The responsibility of carrying Wing Chun forward now rests with us—the current generation of practitioners. Whether you've been studying for decades or just started last week, you're part of this living tradition. Every time you practice, every time you teach or share what you've learned, you're contributing to the legacy of Wing Chun.

But with this responsibility comes a challenge: how do we honor the past while embracing the future? How do we stay true to the art's roots while allowing it to grow and adapt? These aren't easy questions to answer, but they're essential ones.

The Importance of Authenticity

One of the most important things we can do to carry Wing Chun forward is to preserve its authenticity. This doesn't mean resisting change or clinging to tradition for its own sake. It means staying true to the principles that define the art—efficiency, adaptability, balance—while being open to new ideas and perspectives.

Authenticity in Wing Chun isn't about performing the forms exactly as they were taught hundreds of years ago. It's about understanding the purpose behind those forms, the philosophy they represent, and the way they connect to the bigger picture of the art.

As Wing Chun continues to spread and evolve, it's crucial that we keep these principles at the forefront. They are what make Wing Chun unique, what give it its depth and meaning. Without them, the art risks becoming just another set of techniques, disconnected from the philosophy and history that make it so powerful.

Reaching New Audiences

Another key to Wing Chun's future is making it accessible to new audiences. This doesn't just mean attracting more students—it means finding ways to connect with people who might not traditionally consider martial arts.

One of the most exciting developments in recent years has been the integration of Wing Chun into fields like therapy, education, and personal development. Teachers are finding creative ways to use the art's principles to help people build confidence, manage stress, and develop life skills.

For example, some schools are offering programs specifically designed for children, focusing on discipline, focus, and self-control. Others are working with veterans or trauma survivors, using Wing Chun's emphasis on mindfulness and adaptability to help them heal and rebuild.

These efforts show that Wing Chun's relevance goes far beyond the training hall. Its principles can be applied in countless ways, helping people navigate challenges and improve their lives.

Embracing Technology

Technology has already had a significant impact on Wing Chun, and it's likely to play an even bigger role in the years to come. Online classes, video tutorials, and virtual training sessions have made the art more accessible than ever before.

For people who live in areas without local schools, these resources can be a lifeline, allowing them to start learning even if they can't train in person. For advanced practitioners, technology provides opportunities to connect with teachers and peers around the world, sharing insights and refining their skills.

But as with any tool, technology must be used thoughtfully. While it can enhance training, it can't replace the experience of practicing with a live partner or receiving personalized feedback from a teacher. The challenge is finding the right balance—using technology to complement traditional training rather than replacing it.

The Role of Community

If there's one thing that has always been central to Wing Chun, it's the sense of community it creates. From the small groups that practiced in secret centuries ago to the global network of schools and practitioners today, Wing Chun has always been about connection.

This community is one of the art's greatest strengths. It provides support, inspiration, and a sense of belonging. It's where ideas are shared, questions are answered, and progress is celebrated.

As Wing Chun moves forward, this sense of community will be more important than ever. By fostering collaboration and communication among practitioners, we can ensure that the art continues to grow and thrive.

Why Wing Chun Matters

Wing Chun is about more than self-defense or physical fitness. It's about learning how to move through the world with focus, balance, and intention. It's about staying calm under pressure, adapting to change, and finding strength in simplicity.

These lessons are timeless. They were just as relevant in the villages of Southern China centuries ago as they are in the cities and suburbs of today. And they will continue to resonate in the years to come, as long as there are people willing to carry the art forward.

The Endless Journey

One of the most beautiful things about Wing Chun is that it's never finished. There's always more to learn, more to refine, more ways to grow. This sense of endless possibility is part of what makes the art so rewarding.

For those who practice Wing Chun, the journey is its own reward. It's not about reaching a destination or achieving a specific goal—it's about the process, the lessons learned along the way, and the person you become in the process.

As we look to the future of Wing Chun, one thing is clear: its story is far from over. There are still chapters waiting to be written, by practitioners young and old, experienced and new.

The question isn't what's next for Wing Chun—it's what's next for us, the people who practice it. How will we carry its lessons forward? How will we share its principles with others? And how will we continue to grow, both as individuals and as a community?

These are questions worth pondering. Because in the end, Wing Chun isn't just an art—it's a way of life. And its future is in our hands.

Appendix: Resources for Exploring Wing Chun

As you reach the end of this book, you might be feeling inspired to dive deeper into the world of Wing Chun. Whether you're a beginner just getting started or someone with experience looking to expand your understanding, there are countless ways to explore this fascinating art further. This appendix is designed to provide you with practical resources, advice, and guidance to help you on your journey.

Finding a School

The best way to learn Wing Chun is with a qualified teacher. While books and videos can be helpful, there's no substitute for hands-on instruction and personalized feedback. Here are some tips for finding a school or teacher near you:

1. **Start Local**: Use search engines or local directories to look for Wing Chun schools in your area. Visit their websites or social media pages to get a sense of their approach and philosophy.

2. **Attend a Trial Class**: Most schools offer trial classes or free introductory sessions. This is a great opportunity to observe the teaching style, meet the instructors, and get a feel for the

training environment.

3. **Ask Questions**: Don't be afraid to ask questions about the instructor's background, the school's curriculum, and what you can expect as a student. A good teacher will be happy to share their knowledge and experience.

4. **Look for Compatibility**: Not every school will be the right fit for you, and that's okay. Find a teacher and community that align with your goals and values.

Online Resources

If you don't have access to a local school, or if you want to supplement your in-person training, online resources can be incredibly valuable. Here are some options to consider:

1. **Video Tutorials**: Many Wing Chun instructors offer high-quality video tutorials that cover everything from basic techniques to advanced applications. Look for instructors with a strong reputation and clear, detailed teaching

methods.

2. **Virtual Classes**: Some schools offer live virtual classes, allowing you to train with instructors and peers from anywhere in the world. These sessions often include real-time feedback and interaction.

3. **Forums and Communities**: Join online forums, social media groups, or dedicated Wing Chun communities to connect with other practitioners. These platforms can be a great place to ask questions, share experiences, and learn from others.

4. **Apps and Tools**: There are apps available that provide structured Wing Chun training programs, allowing you to practice at your own pace. While these can't replace a teacher, they can be a helpful supplement.

Recommended Reading

If you're interested in the history, philosophy, or techniques of Wing Chun, there are several excellent books available. Look for works written by experienced practitioners who have a deep understanding of the art. Some topics you might explore include:

- The history and evolution of Wing Chun
- Detailed breakdowns of forms and techniques
- The philosophy and principles that underpin the art
- Stories of notable figures who shaped Wing Chun's legacy

Your local library, online retailers, or martial arts specialty shops can be good places to find these resources.

Events and Seminars

Attending Wing Chun events, workshops, or seminars can be a fantastic way to deepen your knowledge and connect with the broader community. These gatherings often feature experienced instructors, demonstrations, and opportunities to train with practitioners from different backgrounds.

Keep an eye out for:

- Local martial arts expos
- Wing Chun seminars hosted by visiting instructors
- International Wing Chun gatherings and conferences

Training Equipment

While Wing Chun doesn't require much equipment, there are a few tools that can enhance your practice:

1. **Wooden Dummy**: The wooden dummy, or Muk Yan Jong, is an iconic training tool in Wing Chun. It helps you develop accuracy, timing, and understanding of angles.

2. **Focus Mitts and Pads**: These are useful for practicing strikes and combinations with a partner.

3. **Protective Gear**: If your training includes sparring, invest in quality protective gear like gloves, headgear, and shin guards.

4. **Training Space**: Whether you're practicing at home or in a gym, create a dedicated space where you can focus on your training without distractions.

Advice for Beginners

Starting Wing Chun can feel overwhelming, especially if you're new to martial arts. Here are some tips to help you get started:

- **Be Patient**: Progress takes time, so don't get discouraged if things don't click right away. Trust the process and focus on small improvements.
- **Ask for Help**: If you're unsure about a technique or principle, don't hesitate to ask your instructor or training partners for clarification.
- **Stay Consistent**: Regular practice is key to building skill and understanding. Even short, daily sessions can make a big difference over time.
- **Embrace the Basics**: Mastery of the fundamentals is what sets the foundation for everything else in Wing Chun. Take your time and focus on getting the basics right.

Staying Inspired

Finally, remember that Wing Chun is a journey, not a destination. There will be times when you feel stuck or frustrated, but those moments are part of the process. Stay curious, stay open, and keep looking for ways to grow.

Talk to fellow practitioners, revisit the principles that drew you to the art in the first place, and celebrate the progress you've made—no matter how small it might seem.

Wing Chun has something to offer everyone, whether you're looking for self-defense, personal growth, or simply a way to stay active. By exploring the resources and opportunities available to you, you can continue to deepen your understanding of this remarkable art and carry its lessons forward in your own life.

Author Bio:
Leighton Tokunbo Shepherd

Leighton Tokunbo Shepherd is a 67-year-old martial artist and teacher who has dedicated over five decades of his life to Judo. Based in Beijing, China, where he's lived most of his life, Shepherd's passion for Judo began as a young man when he first stepped into a small dojo and fell in love with its balance of strength, strategy, and discipline.

Shepherd isn't just someone who practices Judo—he lives it. Over the years, he's competed, taught, and mentored countless students, always focusing on the deeper lessons behind the techniques. To him, Judo is more than a martial art; it's a way of facing life's challenges with confidence and adaptability.

In addition to his work on the mat, Shepherd has spent years reflecting on how the principles of Judo apply to life outside the dojo. Through his teaching and writing, he shares how anyone—whether they practice Judo or not—can benefit from its lessons in resilience, balance, and self-discovery.

Now semi-retired, Shepherd continues to teach in Beijing and is a respected voice in the martial arts community. His straightforward, relatable style makes his insights accessible to everyone, whether they're seasoned martial artists or complete beginners.

From Falling to Flying is his way of sharing what Judo has taught him over a lifetime—about falling, adapting, and thriving, not just in Judo but in life itself.

Made in the USA
Columbia, SC
10 February 2025